T0083424

Monk's Eye

CEES NOOTEBOOM

Monk's Eye
POEMS

TRANSLATED BY DAVID COLMER

WITH DIGITAL COLLAGES BY SUNANDINI BANERJEE

Seagull
BOOKS

LONDON NEW YORK CALCUTTA

Seagull Books, 2018

First published in Dutch as *Monniksoog*
by Karaat in 2016
© Cees Nooteboom, 2016

First published in English by Seagull Books, 2018

English translation © David Colmer, 2018
Digital collages © Sunandini Banerjee, 2018

ISBN 978 0 8574 2 547 8

British Library Cataloguing-in-Publication Data
A catalogue record for this book is available
from the British Library

Book designed by Sunandini Banerjee, Seagull Books
Printed and bound by Maple Press, York, Pennsylvania, USA

Monk's Eye

I

A difficult god on the side of my bed,
six angels with weary wings,
flown in against a gale-force headwind
over the mudflats, a storm at sea.

In the night I see the lights of the opposite shore,
look at the angels who seem to know me and want
to borrow my blanket and actually also the bed,
in which I couldn't sleep anyway.

The god looks like the captain of the ferry,
the rabbits I saw running in the dark
were scared of the hunter, the lighthouse
fell through the room with its beam,

but otherwise everything was fine.

2

I bumped into my mother on the path through the dunes,
she didn't see me. She was talking to another
lady and I heard her say, everyone
likes me here.

I could tell she was real from the sound
of the shells under her feet. Later
I saw my brother and half-brother too,
on their way somewhere with a past the same as mine,

chaos and restlessness. The North Sea had furious breakers,
the beach was deserted. My brothers were transparent.
I saw the path right through them. Now I would like to find a treasure,
a washed-up whale tooth, or gold

to make it all right again.

3

There's not a role in every life for a lighthouse,
but there is in mine. Today on this other island
I walked to the lighthouse, rain, screeching
gulls. At night I got to sit with the keeper,

who acted like he still existed. He wrote it down, a brig
going northabout, the strength of the wind. In the darkness
I saw a light against the waves, and closer by
what he had written in his old-fashioned hand.

Long dead, that keeper. Sailed all the seas, saw all the ports,
Archangel, Valparaiso, the poem by the ship's doctor.
Four on, four off, a night in the lighthouse, a ship
      north-north-west,
silence, smoking, writing, silence, the light over the dunes,

the lighthouse now deserted.

4

Clouds of zinc, fortifications of water, grey,
floating in the light of noon, the sound of waves
and further down the path, two voices, woven
together, tossed up in the air, drawn-out

objections, slow arguments, P. and S.,
raincoats, walking sticks, the language I know from school,
assertions, conclusions among waving marram
and dead brambles. They don't see me, walking past,

going from the dune to the beach,
fine white sand flying to the waves, snow
at their feet. I understand nothing, their words
fly past like sounds and disappear

like froth in the waves.

5

The crow in the birch asked who he was,
but he knew no answer, listening
to the wind in the bushes, looking at his face
in the pond, a moving blur.

The words were speaking at the back of his throat,
but not a one emerged, he heard his name
moving and carried on to the sea
as if he could walk on water.

Around him the singing of a choir,
the wind an instrument that would accompany him.
When he looked back he saw the island the way you see
a ship, a shape disappearing in a bank of fog

that swallows everything.

6

Next to a bush of rosehips I saw
my first love, squatting, like then,
in a doorway. Now I had to choose between
the reality of the bush, the dream of stone,

and kneeling myself, not on the stone of the city
but in the sand of the dunes, a dance
for a man alone. In his arms an illusion, the thin
air of a dead girl who has a voice yet,

the croak of first desire, blown away
and smashed against so many
years, the thistle of not wanting to forget,
take me with you, take me with you,

but where?

7

I bump into everyone here, devils from different
lives, animals from a forgotten coat of arms,
women in the form of lions, unicorns,
masked pigs, I fall out of my painting

and look back at the painter, he still has
to finish my hand, an ant is walking through the paint,
the pianist in the bunker is playing a song
from the war. This is how it all comes back to me,

the dead pilot in the tree, the voice of my
father who could eat on the hoof, I hear his
sound but no words, I know, he wants
to go to his grave but I can't help him.

He hasn't got one.

8

Try it, only words left, no feelings, the power
of them being themselves, you no longer existing,
only listening, language reflected in language.
Feel how you are slowly disappearing, excluded,

you don't belong here and you don't hear them,
you thought you had them, possessed them, servants
or slaves, but they were searching for something else,
letters and sounds you didn't even know about,

you weren't there, driven off because of your abuse,
you had sullied the words, now they would be
realized, inviolable, walled in their own conscience,
their sacred correctness, laws unto themselves,

and out of reach.

9

On the other island it's rocks not dunes,
black, plants with barbs and teeth that drink stone
and cling to grit. Here, too, a lighthouse, high
above the violence of a thunderstorm,

no ships in sight, a hut of stacked stone
for unimaginable people, a vanished species
that lived on sand and water
in a time with no dial.

Now I am flying, I don't need to move my wings, I am
a man of wind, and I see the other me walking down below,
a man like a dog with his nose to the
ground, and I float here with a song between my teeth

that I have never learnt.

On the cliff face a marten
philosopher surprised in his thought,
he abandons his poem,
so I can hear it.

It is about martens,
a dirge in Chinese, about the weight
of the cliff, the roar
of breakers.

In the bay below,
the hunter's knife, the fisherman's house.
I learn the symbols
by heart and write them down

in the sand.

The marten asked, What is evening?
I split myself into a monk,
breathed shadow, no dust on the mirror,
and sought an answer.

Heigh-ho, heigh-ho is, the answer,
as big as a sentence without words.
Never give a poem a difference.
That ends in disaster.

The monk curled up,
a flake of holiness. I know
what I know, said the evening
and disappeared into the cliff face

with no goodbye.

A bird flies, a feather falls.
Incident, the scales of the universe
tip. A fish swims on,
the water ripples, what is now the balance

of the world? The marks are on the
scales, not the world, the question
is multiplied. You are yourself
before you think.

But then? Poems have to get by
without question marks, they have to tame
madness, not deny it, they have to
conjure form from empty thoughts

until they become them.

In the bright daylight, snow glazed with ice,
you might sometimes fall. Go into your enemy's house
and ask who you are. Creeping through the weeds,
your name comes closer.

Is there purpose or portent to this
mirage? Or are they words
that feed on language as movement,
talking to themselves?

Avoid the building of the night,
said the master. What is immediacy?
Touch, the hand on the skin,
the close feeling

that tolerates no further.

14

Thirteen, a number for fog and mist,
direction lost, the road
to the abandoned building,
the location of the dance,

hand in hand, then an extended
sitting and waiting, what is evening,
whose crow is that, whose tortoise,
the fire in the distance?

No answer is always an answer,
later the carp will become a whale,
the small grows large
and cherishes the small

until death comes.

15

A thousand-metre wall, no one in sight.
I cross their land like an ancestor, dreaming their lives.
I know nothing, all I see is imagination.
This is where they walked, smaller than the stones

of their shrines. In the distance the other island,
the one they came from on their ships
of driftwood. Their goddess on board, they laid
their dead on the earth in an upturned

ship of stone. I crawl in over the ground
and hear their whispers. Lies,
I hear nothing, but they are there, asleep in their
body of air, so much nothingness

in this silence.

Phaedrus and S. have turned a corner,
now the wind is blowing towards me, I can
understand them. I hear *rhetoric* and *simple soul*,
I see their gestures. *When he writes he will*

write and sow the garden of letters, says
S. in an old-fashioned translation but
the wind blows away what follows,
leaving snatches of the other voice

saying, *a noble pastime.* They stop for a moment
on the path to light their cigarettes,
but when I take a photo it turns out blank,
a crow flying through emptiness, a northern wood

bathed in light.

That incredibly round blackness, in the soil just last night,
that greyness, silveriness, just pulled from the water,
now seized, cut open, full of blood, still moving,
my food, the man with the knife smiles at me,

we're in it together. Carp with two men,
tableau at the market square, above the door of the town hall
the woman with the sword and the scales, the bells
sounding the angel's message, noon.

I wouldn't say no to another life like this, mud
on my shoes, apples and winter radish in my basket,
crumbled eternity, a hundred metres to go
to the edge of the world, watch out, dreamer,

you'll fall off like a stone.

18

Walker, walker, do you hear us still?
Blue are the mountains, a folding screen,
two men strolling here with four centuries
between them, talking about the soul, how

difficult it is for it to leave the body alone
when it dies, that painstaking home with a stomach
and brains now ruined, ripe for demolition,
and the soul, where to?

You hear those two voices, French, Italian,
in the wind on the country road, you hear the beat
of your steps, the poem of doubt about
the existence of mind, let alone

when it dies.

In a poem of death? One man wrote about
the other long before dawn, long before his time,
poet on painter, and I hear them here on the country road,
because what has been written hangs in the air,

a track to follow, language like spider's web
but spun from steel, thoughts the ear
chafes at, memory's electric fence
encircling the repository of danger,

no, this walk was not free, mirrors are what
they're after, these thinkers, the man with the pen
and the man who cut through a womb, dissected
a coupling, a man who wanted to fly

in a time of not yet.

20

Of all rhythms he found day and night
the most beautiful. One, two, and thank God
no three. That only came later, when
everything was over, a dark number

disguised as a nought. How does a work of art
arise? When does a motet begin,
a poem, a light that seems to have no origin?
Who thinks of a first line before thinking?

From a morass of reflections, a miry
struggle between the past and an invented present,
a single visible moment arises
in which time no longer measures

the sinking.

The laws of inertia, with a line emerging
imperceptibly from a void that requires
something else, but what?
Ask and you will receive, whatever you like.

I want a Russian garden, in a different
century, with an owl in the dark, footsteps in the attic,
a letter from the capital, wind
in tall trees, a faded flag. Past

tense, of course, so everyone
is dead, the garden neglected forever,
an empty swing, glasses left on the table,
the book wet from the rain, where was it, when

in my absence?

Think up a past, do not skimp
on war or infidelity. Your father at sea,
on deck, young, spats, a trench coat,
a silent film without a title,

a man on his way to the Orient, something
or other 1920, a nameless ship
and nothing left to ask. There is no code
for remembering the dead,

nobody lives there. Empty wardrobes, the empty
house that is a name. I watch the man
on deck, does he hear the sea? Does he hear
the sea like I do now? An old man

he never saw.

23

Night ride, the same road as always, you know the bends,
now painted black. The dog's usual corner is gloomy,
thoughts of the dog already obliterated, the stables
gone, the darkness denying the wood.

Someone spoke of guilt,
but it was about us,
deception beyond the capabilities of nature,
our origin the first matter,

stardust, grit that became flesh, that
uses words and destroys them too,
removing itself from the mirror
because there is no light

to see anyone.

24

My brother ravine, my sister torrent,
my mother reeds for a hut, my father lichen
on rust-coloured rocks, his father family to fish,
waterborne with lungs, like you.

No one thought us up, we were in the grit
of the first second, we have been here from
the beginning. Only later did we get souls and were
we allowed to write. Ours are the words

of stone and water. Never have we
denied our origin, we are what is,
numbers with a nothing on the end. Once someone threw
a stone in the water, those ever-widening circles,

even now, are us.

25

It seemed so simple, the house
as space, you an earth and I
an unequivocal moon, visible
and then invisible again,

but always circling you. I was the light
for poets and fishers who wanted
to belong to you, I determined the sea
as movement, nestling up

to every coast as surf,
always thinking of you,
a heavenly body, together
and always alone, with an eternal

back and forth.

On the shell path, that old friend. His clothes,
which I recognized, were holding together
the empty space he had been. The friend loved
choral music. I hear it now, Tenebrae

across the beach and the sea, so grey
and dangerous, the colours of almost dead.
The friend walked slowly, moved
his hands, stopped to look back

but didn't see me. I followed the empty
figure until I had caught up to him. His absent body
was humming the melody I recognized.
I didn't dare speak. I didn't know the language

he would understand.

27

Why don't the dead leave us in peace?
They scatter their names over the road
we have to walk, insert their lines of verse
in our last bit of sleep before morning,

then go again, absent as if
it's a profession, turning away, eyeless,
hidden in their own jargon, the private
dialect of the dead, inaccessible

to us, a race that's stateless and voiceless
and breaks into our memories
without appointments, walking next to us
or sitting on the side of the bed where they

once lay.

28

Because there was nothing there, everything
absent, a dark lack, the question
for the swan on the black water
was why.

The swan spoke of its form
as the only truth, but the man, in the form
of his shadow, waited for more, the taste
of an answer against the darkness

for which there were no words.
They stood like that for hours without moving, swan
against man, man against swan. The poem
they became made itself in silence,

but without a language.

29

That was how they saw themselves from a distance,
an elevation, as others. But the sound of the sea
remained the same for those strangers,
Tenebrae, hallucinations,

mirrors that were home to others
who no longer wanted to live,
scarecrows in the dunes, faces
hidden in marram, sailed off

beyond the last buoy, in legends of sand-hills
and banks, whispering of Willemsduin
in the waves over Wantij and Rif,
a slumber chain of names and forgetting

in which you disappear.

30

Back to the island where the words first
emerged from the case of letters
I've lugged around my whole life long. Wind, first light,
the morning full of bird talk, warblers, avocets

grebes, a language I don't speak, that I hear.
Those I see have no substance, egg capsules on the beach,
varnished armour of vanished animals, the thorny
skate, necklace shells, among them ghosts,

my dead companions, invisible
beside me on our way to the Balg, where the land
turns to water, a gleaming surface
on which they walk to the word

on the horizon.

31

In the end the old poet wanted nothing more
to do with the sea. Something so wide and open
terrified him, he said, he saw his
transparent life in a transparent

death. A ship no longer helped,
it was an accent on emptiness, rowed
by a nobody, a ghost without hands,
bird-shaped, bent forward

as if there were still land, a port.
If he still spoke it was in fables,
descent to the underworld,
his old friends' last home, now

without a voice.

32

A feast for beachcombers, the wind and its instruments,
the rip in the sail. On the sand you find everything
dancing in the froth, angel's wings,
a comb, a dog's back almost of gold,

your past without the names, a mother,
an oar and a rudder, the storm shrieks
under the beach cabin, seaweed around
the mooring post, barnacles anchored to the wood,

and against the night sky the spoils,
who you wanted to become and who you never became,
not you, in the false colours of passion,
ready for the celebrations, where you will get to be

the beachcomber.

33

Night on the coast. The moon fleeing,
a lover in tatters. How did you think
it would end? Over the dunes the twins approach,
women of great beauty,

heads shaved. Coming straight from
your childhood, they are part of the secret, them
and the thorn bush that flies past your feet,
a wind-harried father, the woman you wanted.

Was this all? And then Orion too, high
and disfigured, your friend in this sole
existence. He gropes his way blindly in the dark
to the murmur of the sea, in which his dog

has drowned.

The murmur of the sea,
the murmur of the sea,

the murmur of the sea

Monk's Eye

An I who is a he, a him who is me, images of an island that becomes another island (an archetypal *insula*), and then itself again. Dream images drawn from reality, Phaedrus and Socrates on the path through the dunes, and later Valéry and da Vinci, who never knew each other, talking to the wind. How much must you tell or explain, how many secrets that went into the making are you allowed to keep for yourself if you think they were essential?

While writing this poem, from December 2015 to April 2016, I called it 'Schiermonnikoog', because it was on a December night on that Dutch island that the beginning came to me, taking me by surprise. Schiermonnik-oog, island (oog = eye) of the grey monks (Cistercians). Luc de Roy, the original publisher of this poem, suggested 'Monnikoog', to avoid misunderstandings, as the poem is, of course, not explicitly about that West Frisian island, even if it could not have existed without it. I made it *Monniksoog, Monk's Eye,* if only because I was once educated by monks and my first contact with really great poetry stems from those days—monastery gymnasiums, Ovid, Homer, Virgil,

an inescapable part of me. But also because that grey monk is central to the island's coat of arms; you see him everywhere, like the sea itself. It's like that on islands.

Images, illusions, dreams. Schiermonnikoog and the other island I spend part of my life on, Minorca. Always the surrounding sea, lighthouses, ferries, the world always at a distance, and a different world of my own here as a result. And the essence of all poetry in the first line of the *Phaedrus,* when Socrates, walking with his admirer, asks him: 'My dear Phaedrus, whence come you, and whither are you going?'

CN